DISHWASHER LOADING DECRYPTED

— THE ART OF STACKING —

HAYDEN WALSH

I Create from the Heart
Melbourne, Australia
www.icreatefromtheheart.com

ISBN 978-1-7638278-0-6

Disclaimer

The information provided in this book is intended for general guidance, educational purposes, and, most importantly, satire. The author and publisher have made every effort to ensure the accuracy and effectiveness of the tips and techniques described; however, they make no guarantees regarding specific results or outcomes.

Readers are advised to refer to the user manual and safety instructions provided by the manufacturer of their dishwasher before operating the appliance. Proper care and maintenance of your dishwasher, as recommended by the manufacturer, are essential for safe and effective use.

The author and publisher disclaim any liability for any damage, injury, loss or heated household debates resulting from the use or misuse of the information provided in this book. Readers should exercise caution, a sense of humour and personal judgment when applying the suggestions presented and seek professional advice if needed. Or at least consult someone who actually has read the manual.

By reading this book, you acknowledge and agree that the author and publisher cannot be held responsible for any consequences resulting from actions taken based on its contents. If this book causes you to rethink your entire approach to dishwasher loading, you're welcome.

Dedicated to my lovely wife, Jo, with everlasting hope that one day she will learn to stack the dishwasher the way I do.

CONTENTS

FOREWORD

By the Missus

After many years of practicing and perfecting his dishwasher stacking skills, my loving husband, Hayden, has decided it was time to share his prowess and take his expert knowledge into the world.

He has been frustrated by the complete lack of care and judgement when others take on the momentous task of stacking the dishwasher. There are many ways you can get it wrong, and Hayden is here to show you the way.

Enjoy his conversational teaching style as he guides you, with informative tips, holding back his frustration, hoping one day you can get it right.

Listen in horror as he recalls tales of where it has gone wrong and the disastrous results, including bowls turned upside down and filled with water, utensils that weren't cleaned properly, and—worst of all—rewashing a full load.

1.

BACKGROUND

Since the beginning of time, humans have been thinking about how they can clean their dishes in the most effective way, given their circumstances. This potential novel will provide valuable advice, as our time is forever being eroded by multiple factors in our everyday lives. Summarising into a manual that will provide a happy ending for everybody—and stop those awkward arguments about who stacked the dishwasher incorrectly, which could, if not corrected, lead to divorce.

In the last 100 years there have been significant advances in the way we clean our dishes. From the first electric dishwasher made by Miele in 1929 to having permanent plumbing available, it was not until the postwar boom of the 1950s that things really took off.

Combined with the fact that women's rights have meant more equality in the running of most households—and that child labour is now "limited"—has meant lots of interesting family kitchen banter has developed on how to stack a dishwasher in the most effective way, without having to rewash dishes, or, worse still, replace broken items.

Like a car, your dishwasher also needs regular servicing and maintenance to ensure it runs as efficiently and lasts as long as possible. It can cause issues if not looked after and can lead to some expensive repairs. I have included a service checklist at the end of the manual.

I treat the stacking as a game involving mathematics and dexterity, where optimisation to meet an outcome is the challenge. My inspiration came from old arcade games like *Galaga* and *Donkey Kong*, where a set pattern had to be followed to get to the next level. This manual is a little over-engineered for most stackers, but I think my computational patterns will provide the ideal directive for the average stacker.

This manual will delve into some stories that most families have encountered and will provide risk-avoidance strategies, issue management, assumptions, dependencies, and a quiz at the end. If you pass the quiz, there is also a certificate that you can proudly show your friends and family.

2.

STORIES

In households with dishwashers, there are many discussions about how the dishwasher has been stacked. Here are some of those stories.

The most common story I have heard is that of the flipped plastic container: The horror of finding out that a family member had carelessly placed an object, with no thought process at all, to the detriment of the whole family ecosystem. This can lead to deep psychological impacts if this is an ongoing problem and not corrected immediately.

Trips back to my birth country of New Zealand often bring gasps of exasperation as I inspect how my wife's family stacks the dishwasher. I shudder to think how any of them get clean, given the way they are stacked. The photo (right) is a classic example of hoping for the best. I went to help finish stacking the dishwasher and found wine glasses stacked sideways. I guess this would clean the outside, but the inside would have next to no chance.

One time, we had a guest who insisted on doing the dishes after dinner. Their technique was interesting. They started by filling the sink first and handwashing the dishes before putting them in the dish-

washer. It sounds reasonable, as this would remove the bulk of the excess food remains, right? No, this leaves nothing for the dishwashing tablet to adhere to. It might look like the dishes come out clean, but you've wasted a bit of water in the process, not to mention time.

Another example from New Zealand is that of the grater being used for garlic and ginger. Ginger, especially, gets stuck into the smaller-holed graters and should always be hand-washed. As seen in the photograph below, the dishwasher had no chance of cleaning this grater. And yes, in case you are wondering, this is after the cycle was completed.

Being an ex-uni student, I have seen disposable plastic plates, bowls, cups, and cutlery being put in the dishwasher. Very cost-effective if you don't have the budget, but I have seen these melt under high temperatures. Not checking the washing instructions on items can lead to major problems. Are you supposed to wash takeaway containers? How many of you actually do that?

When unstacking the cutlery basket, I cut my finger on a sharp knife that somebody had purposely placed upwards, as some sort of revenge. The immediate blame always falls on the same person from whom you need to get the Band-Aid and sympathy from. This can be worse than getting a paper cut, which, as we know, is one of the most pathetically painful injuries one can endure.

Finding dirty cutlery in the drawer when setting the dinner table is an issue. Why did the person unstacking the dishwasher not notice? What happened to quality control? Does someone in the household need training or new spectacles? So many questions go through the mind. Such mishaps, whether with dirty cutlery or malfunctioning kitchen tools, make us wonder: What else can go wrong with the dishwasher?

Ever wondered why your tongs stopped working? Could it be that the dishwasher has stolen the springs? I have seen this a few times when cleaning the filter. Once the dishwasher stopped cleaning altogether, which I suspect was due to a small metal part, ending up past the filter and venturing into the deep unknown. This cost half the price of the dishwasher to fix.

Another mind-boggling act is when visitors change the settings to make the dishwasher wash quicker. This is often caused by well-meaning relatives, but touching the settings of another person's device is heavily frowned upon—unless it works better, of course.

Once upon a time, I used to turn the dishwasher on before going to bed at night to take advantage of the lower cost of off-peak power usage. One morning, I got up for work to find the kitchen floor flooded, as the outflow pipe had become unsecured. This left a big cleanup job and some floor and wall damage, which could have been a lot worse. Now we have solar panels, so we've switched to maximising use of power during the day.

And the worst-case scenario is when you turn on the dishwasher and don't realise you've forgotten the detergent. Then, upon unstacking, you notice clues that something has gone wrong, and you have to rewash the load. Performing a root cause analysis can be challenging, as the blame game can expand into household disputes about who does the most work around the home.

3.

RISKS

There are multiple inherent risks with stacking a dishwasher. Some people don't even realise that these risks exist and stack with wild abandonment, giving no thought to the outcome. Here is a list of potential risks to consider and how you can mitigate these risks.

- **Lack of Placement**: Location of items is very important. Ensure items are placed with the dirty side of the object facing toward the middle. This enables the most amount of water from the spray arm to wash the dish.

- **Cracking**: Delicate glasses, especially those with stems, packed too closely together may expand under the heat of the dishwasher and crack. Do not place glasses or cups on top of the tines, as they are designed to separate items and prevent them from knocking into each other or falling over.

- **Crystal**: Crystal should never be cleaned in a dishwasher. It is typically a higher-priced item, and the risk of attacking crystal items with extreme temperatures and harsh detergents can cause it to become cloudy and lose any decorative elements like gold or silver trims. Always mitigate this risk by handwashing.

- **Plastics**: Plastic items should not be placed on the bottom rack as the heat is higher and may damage the items. Obviously, disposable plastic plates, bowls, and cutlery are not designed to be placed in a dishwasher. Unless otherwise indicated, right?

- **Wooden Items**: Items that are wooden should not be added to the dishwasher at all. This includes wooden chopping boards, steak knives, and cheese knives with wooden handles. Wood can split and fade in hot water. It can also break apart, causing debris in the filter.

- **Resin Bowls**: The heat can warp and ruin the product. Avoid this at all costs.

- **Rinsing**: An interesting topic. Obviously, solids need to be removed before placing items in the dishwasher. But a rinse of the dishes in the sink is generally not recommended. This is because the detergent needs something to grab onto, in order to clean as designed. Most dishwashers have a turbidity sensor that measures the level of soil in the first rinse, so if you pre-rinse your dishes, it will use less power, and dishes might come out dirtier. The only exceptions are rinsing off extra salt, as it can scratch glassware and is corrosive to metal; and chia seeds, which can block the filter as they expand with water. You may have your own items that are blacklisted as well.

- **Prevention of Optimal Water Flow**: Leave a gap between plates and bowls to allow water and detergent to reach all areas. Most modern appliances will also have a height adjustment for the top shelves so that larger plates on the bottom shelves will not be hit by the water arm, which washes the top tray. Test with your dishwasher on larger items to ensure the risk is minimised as per photo below.

- **Rinse Aid**: Always use rinse aid. Some detergents include rinse aid but always ensure the rinse aid dispenser is filled, as it improves drying and reduces water spots and filming.

- **Detergents**: Do your research on these or experiment to find one that suits your budget as detergent can be expensive. The cheapest is not always the most effective and may contain harsh abrasive agents that can dull or wear away your delicate glassware.

- **Half-full Washing**: Some users wash a half load. Dishwashers are made to run on a full load, so this wastes energy and water. Additionally, a full dishwasher will have a better drying performance because of the greater thermal mass of its contents.

- **Overloading**: The evil nemesis stacker overloads their dishwasher just to prove a point. This is highly risky. Badly stacked and overloaded dishwashers can block the jets and prevent detergent from cleaning optimally.

- **Filters**: Ensure the filters are cleaned once a month to get maximum efficiency; otherwise, you risk soap residue or food particles accumulating, which can also create odours. In the worst case, you risk blocking the filter, which can cause issues with drainage or damage the pump.

- **Labels**: Ensure new items have had their labels or stickers removed, or you risk them coming off and blocking the filter.

- **Moveable Parts**: Do not include any item with a movable part, such as tongs with springs. Over time, the spring will corrode and fall apart, leaving small washers or springs at the mercy of the filter.

- **Knives**: Ensure sharp knives are placed downward in the cutlery basket, or you may receive a nasty cut. Carving knifes should always be hand-washed, as dishwashers can cause them to become blunt over time.

- **Baking Dishes**: Generally these items carry too many risks to place in the dishwasher, as detergent and water can damage them over time. Keep it simple and hand-wash them. Exceptions include ceramic baking dishes and silicon bakeware.

- **Household Items**: I've seen some interesting items placed in the dishwasher, like toys, combs, sponges, and flip-flops, but I would suggest handwashing these items, as it's not always clear if they are dishwasher-safe.

4.

ISSUES

If you have failed to manage some of the risks, then here are some issues that may arise in the day-to-day fiascos of a poorly trained dishwasher stacker, along with ideas to mitigate them from happening again.

- **Upside-down Bowls**: The enemy of the professional stacker. The disgust of finding a bowl filled with water can bring the strongest man or woman to their lowest point. If this persists for an extended period, ensure psychiatric help is sought. For the amateur stacker, keep practising until the training leads to rewards.

- **Broken Glasses**: When these items are found, they can be costly if it is an ongoing theme. Always check through the dishwasher to locate all remnants and ensure glasses are stacked carefully in the future.

- **Rust spots**: Monitor the cutlery for any spots. This can be due to cheap cutlery, long exposure to oxygen and water, or residual steam in the appliance. The best option to reduce rust spots is to open the dishwasher after it has finished,

and don't add items that have rust on them. Some dishwashers now feature an automatic door-opening function when the cycle is complete.

- **Serving Spoon Pooling**: If you are not careful, items such as large spoons that are not placed facing down will pool with water and not clean properly, as shown to the right.

- **Lipstick**: In the past, old dishwashers and detergent could not handle lipstick very well. Although this issue is less prevalent today, it can still appear. In this case below, the issue was caused by a large plate on the lower tray blocking the washing arm and not cleaning the load properly.

- **Tissues**: Occasionally, I've found a tissue in the bottom of the dishwasher. This is usually because the tissue was stuck on the bottom of a plate and made its way into the dishwasher unnoticed. Check the bottom of plates and bowls when stacking.

5.

ASSUMPTIONS

There are basic assumptions that are general knowledge in the dishwashing expert stackers community. In case you are not part of this community, I have listed a few items below.

- **Basic Stacking of Plates**: Ensure large plates are placed on the outside and face inwards on the bottom shelf. A cycle will have the best result if dishes mimic the shape of the dishwasher's spray arm. If possible, place the dirtiest dishes in the middle to receive the best spray from the arm.

- **Basic Stacking of Glasses**: Glasses should be placed on the top shelf. They can break easily, so avoid placing them near heavy objects that may move.

- **Cutlery Placement**: If you have a basket, it is recommended to place items with their handles up. This makes it easier and more hygienic to remove. Just ensure that items like spoons are not caught "spooning," as this can cause repeated cleaning and angst amongst unstackers. A cutlery tray above the top rack is even better, as it makes it easier to separate and unstack.

- **Handy Tips**: Other items that can be placed in the dishwasher are microwave turntables, fridge shelving, and even your stainless steel range hood filter. Also, avoid buying plates that are too big. You may need to ensure the rotating arm can spin freely with larger objects.

- **Pots and Pans**: These items need to be checked to see if they are dishwasher-safe. Cast iron, enamelled cast iron, non-stick, and most aluminium items should not be placed in the dishwasher. To be on the safe side, I would hand wash these items, as the harsh dishwasher detergents can cause them to turn dull, darken, pit, and corrode over time.

- **Occasional Users**: Some people don't have enough dishes to run the dishwasher daily. Beware that items like egg, some cereals, and avocado can become harder to wash. In worse cases, items will grow mould, which is not ideal. To avoid this, ensure you wash as frequently as possible.

- **Open After Use**: Once the cycle has completed, the door should be opened to allow proper drying. This will reduce the rust spots on cutlery and help prevent mould, especially on the seals. I suggest using the appliance during the day, especially if you have solar panels.

6.

DEPENDENCIES

Tips to ensure the most efficient clean.

- **Rinsing**: Not required for the modern dishwasher. Rinsing wastes water, and if dishes are too clean, they may not wash properly.

- **Full Load**: Wait until you get a full load to get maximum efficiency.

- **Temp**: The perfect temperature for washing is 60°C. Check your dishwasher's settings to select the closest temperature to this.

- **Over-stacking**: Don't overload, which is my pet peeve. This can cause some dishes not to clean properly.

- **Unstacking**: When unloading the dishwasher, start with the bottom rack to prevent drips from the top rack. To reduce drips from the top rack, ensure plastics are secured so they don't flip and become a miniature swimming pool. Place cups on an angle so water can run off them. Note that some cups have a groove on the underside for water to run off more effectively.

7.

EXAMPLES

Added below are some ideal layouts as a guide for stacking your dishwasher.

- **Cutlery Tray**: If your dishwasher comes with a cutlery tray, it is very handy. It cleans your cutlery more consistently as you can reduce the amount of "spooning" and you are not restricted by the size of a cutlery basket. It is also far easier to unstack if the forks, knives, and spoons are placed beside each other. Pictured here is a layout I use, but this can be adapted to whatever pattern suits. As the picture shows, the grooves are to keep the top of the forks and spoons in place and determine the direction of the cutlery.

- **Middle Layer**: This is typically reserved for glasses, cups, plastics, and large cutlery items. This tray is standard, and it helps to have similarly sized glasses and cups so you don't have to adjust the height of the tray, if you have the option. Example below.

Big glasses, cups and plastic containers.

Big utensils and odd shaped items.

Standard sized glasses, cups.

- **Bottom Tray**: This level requires heavy-duty cleaning. Ensure items are not touching, as the spray arms are angled specifically for each dishwasher to enable the most effective cleaning. Grouping similar items together also makes it easier to unstack.

8.

HANDY HINTS

Some users tend forget how to stack a dishwasher immediately after being shown. To help with this I have added some reminders.

- **Posters**: Showing examples around the kitchen as reminders, such as the one in this image. This reminder may drive the amateur stacker crazy, but over time, they will become more proficient, and it can be removed once they achieve the level of the chief stacker of the household. Note that this should only occur once the chief stacker agrees that proficiency has been reached.

- **Picture frames**: Another idea is to put photos in a picture frame and display them around the kitchen, lounge, or even in the bedroom as a reminder to your loved ones. In fact, stacking a dishwasher can be considered an art form, so displaying it in a frame is ideal.

- **Flowchart**: For the complete novice, a basic flowchart displayed prominently in the kitchen may help. This is especially useful for teenagers, office workers, housemates, and the rebel dishwasher stacker.

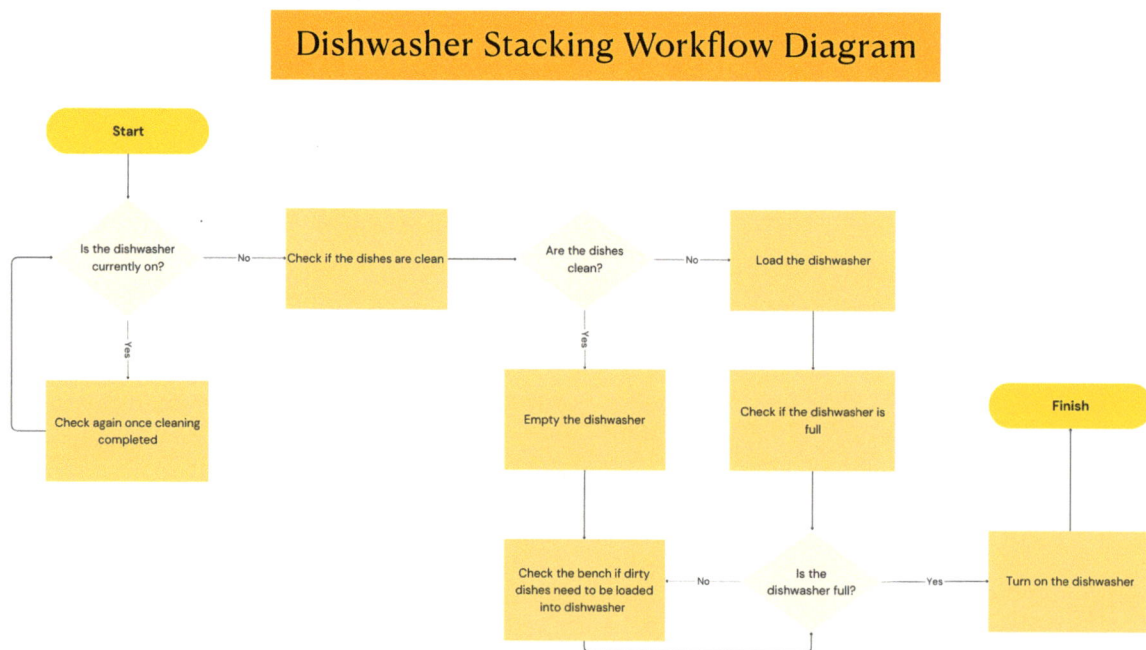

Dishwasher Stacking Workflow Diagram

Start

Is the dishwasher currently on?

No → Check if the dishes are clean → Are the dishes clean?

No → Load the dishwasher

Yes → Check again once cleaning completed

Yes → Empty the dishwasher

Check if the dishwasher is full

Check the bench if dirty dishes need to be loaded into dishwasher

No ← Is the dishwasher full? → Yes → Turn on the dishwasher

Finish

9.

QUIZ

T o ensure you have thoroughly read this manual, here are a few questions to pon-
der. You will need to score 100% on the test to pass and receive your certificate.

- What is the ideal temperature for your dishwasher to be set to?

- Should you place a wooden spoon in the dishwasher?

- How many issues can you see in this stack?

- Why is rinse aid typically blue?

- In what year was the first electric dishwasher made?

- Should you place disposable plastic plates in the dishwasher?

ABOUT THE AUTHOR

Hayden is a highly qualified individual with multiple certificates to prove he is good at what he does. Originally from a small farming town in New Zealand, he enjoys chocolate and considers himself a professional armchair athlete. With a background in cleanliness, a knack for predicting worst-case scenarios, and competitive in any challenge, he dreamed of one day writing about his observations to help others improve their daily well-being.

Service checks should be made at least once a month to keep your appliance in tip-top condition. Check your manual for instructions.

FILTER CHECK/CLEAN

Date:

Who:

Notes:

FILTER CHECK/CLEAN

Date:

Who:

Notes:

FILTER CHECK/CLEAN

Date:

Who:

Notes:

FILTER CHECK/CLEAN

Date:

Who:

Notes:

FILTER CHECK/CLEAN

Date:

Who:

Notes:

FILTER CHECK/CLEAN

Date:

Who:

Notes:

FILTER CHECK/CLEAN

Date:

Who:

Notes:

FILTER CHECK/CLEAN

Date:

Who:

Notes:

FILTER CHECK/CLEAN

Date:

Who:

Notes:

FILTER CHECK/CLEAN

Date:

Who:

Notes:

FILTER CHECK/CLEAN

Date:

Who:

Notes:

FILTER CHECK/CLEAN

Date:

Who:

Notes:

CERTIFICATE

OF COMPLETION

This certifies that

....

has successfully completed the training
programme requirement for

MASTERY IN HOW TO STACK THE DISHWASHER

Hayden Walsh

INSTRUCTOR

DATE

www.ingramcontent.com/pod-product-compliance
Lightning Source LLC
LaVergne TN
LVHW072122070426
835511LV00002B/58